W9-AGM-933

All About Your
SKIN

Jenny Fretland VanVoorst
and Maria Koran

www.av2books.com

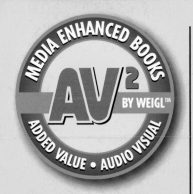

AV² provides enriched content that supplements and complements this book. Weigl's AV² books strive to create inspired learning and engage young minds in a total learning experience.

Your AV² Media Enhanced books come alive with...

Audio
Listen to sections of the book read aloud.

Key Words
Study vocabulary, and complete a matching word activity.

Video
Watch informative video clips.

Quizzes
Test your knowledge.

Go to **www.av2books.com**, and enter this book's unique code.

Embedded Weblinks
Gain additional information for research.

Slide Show
View images and captions, and prepare a presentation.

BOOK CODE

N452975

AV² **by Weigl** brings you media enhanced books that support active learning.

Try This!
Complete activities and hands-on experiments.

... and much, much more!

Published by AV² by Weigl
350 5ᵗʰ Avenue, 59ᵗʰ Floor
New York, NY 10118
Website: www.av2books.com

Library of Congress Cataloging-in-Publication Data

Names: Fretland VanVoorst, Jenny, 1972- author. | Koran, Maria, author.
Title: Skin / Jenny Fretland VanVoorst and Maria Koran.
Description: New York, NY : AV2 by Weigl, [2017] | Series: All about your...
| Includes bibliographical references and index.
Identifiers: LCCN 2016034652 (print) | LCCN 2016035186 (ebook) | ISBN
 9781489651525 (hard cover : alk. paper) | ISBN 9781489651532 (soft cover :
 alk. paper) | ISBN 9781489651549 (Multi-user ebk.)
Subjects: LCSH: Skin--Juvenile literature.
Classification: LCC QM484 .F74 2017 (print) | LCC QM484 (ebook) | DDC
 612.7/9--dc23
LC record available at https://lccn.loc.gov/2016034652

Printed in the United States of America in Brainerd, Minnesota
1 2 3 4 5 6 7 8 9 0 20 19 18 17 16

082016
210716

Project Coordinator: Piper Whelan   Art Director: Terry Paulhus

2   All About Your

Contents

Chapter 1
The Skin You Are In

Have you ever heard of your birthday suit? This term refers to your skin. It is what you were wearing when you were born. It is funny, but it is true. Your skin is a suit of armor that protects what is inside.

Skin is the largest **organ** in the body. An adult's skin when stretched out is the size of a twin bed sheet. It would weigh as much as an 8-pound (4-kilogram) house cat. Skin can be thin like the skin on your eyelids. It can also be thick like the soles of your feet.

The skin on the bottom of the feet can develop callouses.
A callous is an area of skin that is thick and tough.

Touch is important for human growth. Studies show babies need to be held and cuddled.

Skin has many important jobs. Skin keeps your insides in your body. It also keeps objects on the outside from going into your body. Skin forms a wall. It keeps water and **germs** away from your internal organs. It also keeps out the cold. Your skin keeps your body warm inside even when it is freezing outside. Your skin also protects your body against overheating by sweating. A healthy body has an internal temperature of 98.6 degrees Fahrenheit (37 degrees Celsius).

Your skin is also the organ where you can feel the sense of touch. Imagine going to the beach. You feel the crunch of sand between your toes. The sun makes your shoulders warm. The waves splash on your legs. Your body is covered with skin, so you can feel with all parts of your body.

When you are very active, the body heats up. Physical activity causes you to sweat, which keeps the skin and body cool.

Chapter 2

Get Under Your Skin

Take a look in the mirror. Does your skin look healthy and bright? Think again. Everything you see is dead skin.

The top layer of your skin is made of dead skin **cells**. This thin layer is called the **epidermis**. New skin cells form at the bottom of the epidermis. Then, they move upward. As skin cells die, they are pushed together and flattened. This is the skin you see. These dead skin cells overlap like shingles on a roof. They form a protective wall for the tissues beneath. You are always shedding these dead skin cells. In one minute you may lose up to 40,000 skin cells.

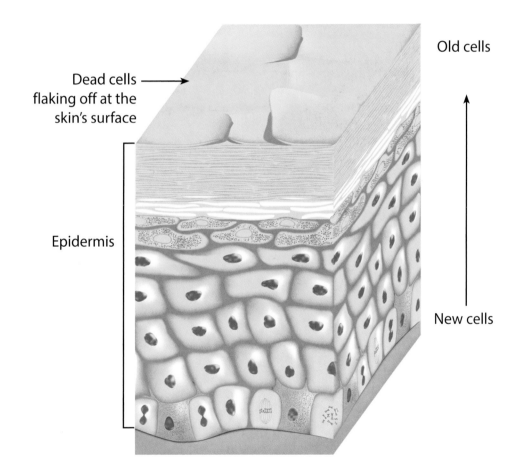

Dead cells flaking off at the skin's surface

Old cells

Epidermis

New cells

A skin cell lives for about 35 days. The cell is created and sheds in this time. In one year you will have shed more than 12 sets of skin.

The epidermis is covered in an oily coating. This coating is like a raincoat. It keeps water from going into the body. However, this raincoat is not completely waterproof. Your skin will absorb some water. Do you like to go swimming? Are your fingers and toes wrinkly afterward? That is what happens when your skin absorbs water.

The epidermis is very thin, like a page in a book. Underneath the epidermis is a thicker layer called the **dermis**. The dermis houses blood vessels, sweat **glands**, and nerve endings. Blood vessels help your skin keep an even temperature. They increase or decrease blood flow to the surface of the skin. Sweat glands cool the skin by releasing sweat.

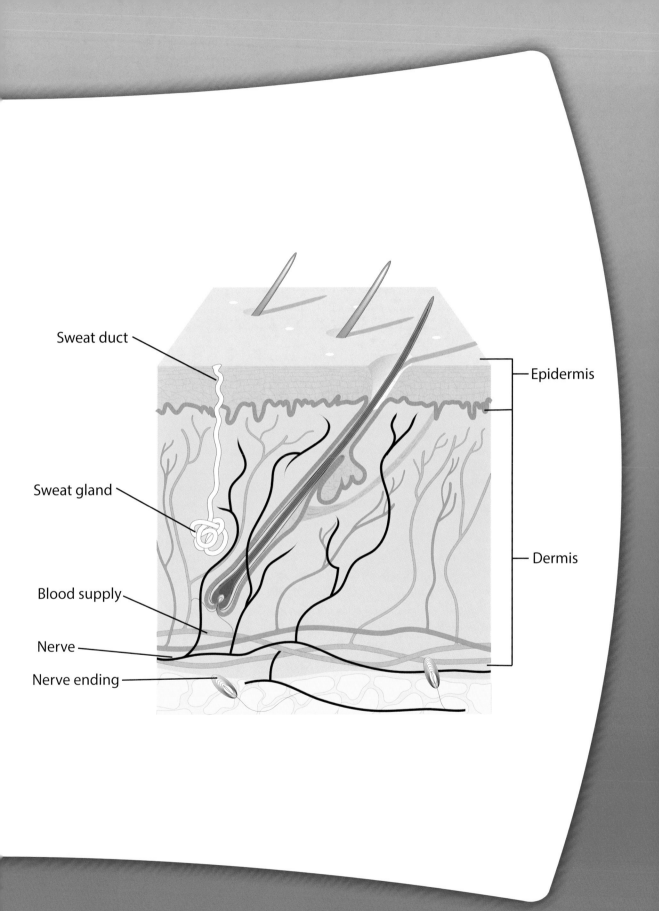

Sweat duct

Sweat gland

Blood supply

Nerve

Nerve ending

Epidermis

Dermis

Nerve endings give you the sense of touch. The nerves end in sensors that work together. The sensors detect texture, pressure, movement, temperature, itchiness, and pain. A million sensors fit in an area the size of your fingernail. When you burn yourself, these sensors detect both heat and pain. They send a message through the nerves to the brain. The brain decodes the message. It sends your muscles a message to move away from the source of the pain. Nerve cells allow you to feel a painful burn. They also allow you to feel a cat's soft fur.

Fingertips have more nerve endings than anywhere else on the body.

There are about 2,500 nerve receptors in an area the size of a raindrop on the human hand.

Chapter 3

When Good Skin Goes Bad

Your skin works hard to protect you. Sometimes, skin hurts or is cut. Pain is the first sign something is wrong. Pain is a **signal** that cells have been damaged. Do not ignore this signal. You might hurt your skin more. Delaying care might also make a wound harder to heal.

Cuts and scrapes are common injuries. You might get a cut from a sharp knife. You might also scrape your knee on the sidewalk. Your amazing skin will heal itself over time. Skin cells multiply and rush to seal up the wound. Most cuts and scrapes do not go deeper than the epidermis. They can be cleaned and covered with a bandage. If the cut is very large or deep, you may need stitches. A doctor will fix your skin like you might fix a torn shirt.

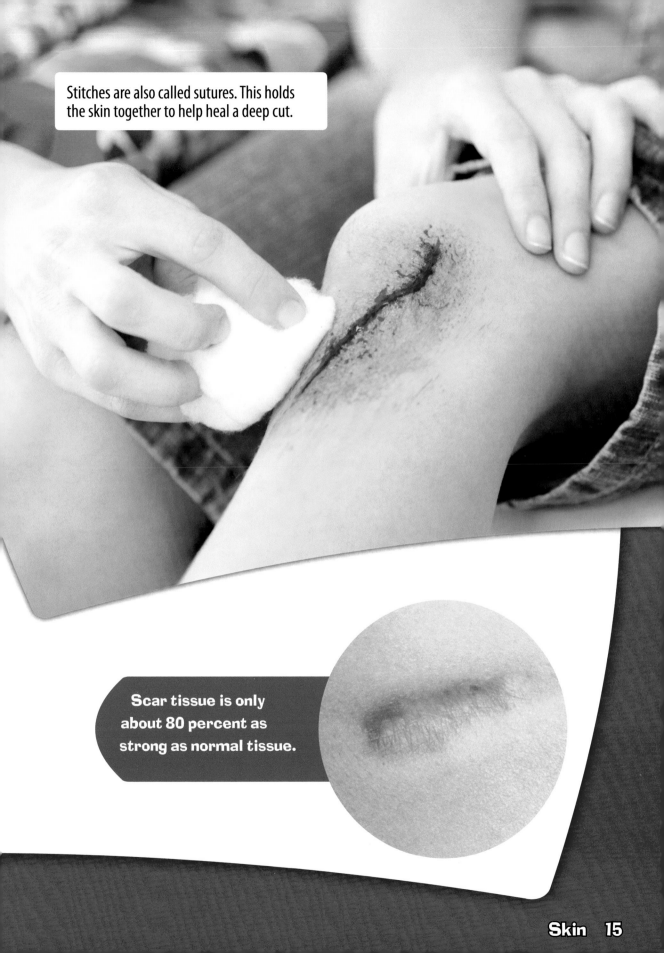

Stitches are also called sutures. This holds the skin together to help heal a deep cut.

Scar tissue is only about 80 percent as strong as normal tissue.

Sunburn is also a common problem. Skin burns if it is in the sun too long. It becomes red and sore. Sometimes, it peels. Once again, your amazing skin works to protect itself. **Melanin** is a substance your skin makes. This substance protects your skin from the sun's damaging rays. Melanin causes your skin to tan. Darker skin has more melanin than lighter skin. Sometimes, the sun burns before enough melanin can be made. You get a sunburn. A sunburn does not just hurt. It can damage your skin and lead to more serious problems.

Sunburns hurt, but they can also make you sick. It is important to wear sunscreen or sun clothing to protect your skin.

Some plants, such as poison ivy, can give the skin a bad, itchy rash. It is important to wear long pants when hiking.

Have you ever touched a plant like poison ivy? You probably ended up with red, blistering, and itchy skin. The plant's sap irritates the skin and causes a rash. Scented laundry detergent can cause some people's skin to itch. Certain drugs can have an effect on your skin, too. Steer clear of things you know will irritate you. Your skin will thank you for it.

Chapter 4
Skin Deep

Your skin does a good job of taking care of itself. There are some things you can do to help make its job easier.

Keep your skin clean. It comes in contact with dirt and germs during the day. Wash it with soap and water. Then, pat it dry rather than rubbing.

Treat cuts and scrapes gently. Clean the wound and cover it with an **antibiotic** cream. Then, cover it with a bandage to protect it. Do not pick scabs. They are part of the healing process.

People in many cultures decorate their skin as a way to express themselves. Makeup, tattoos, and piercings are some of the more common methods.

The skin on your hands can spread germs easily. Washing your hands is a good way to stay healthy.

To avoid sunburn, wear sunscreen when you are outside. You can get a sunburn even when it is cloudy. Choose a sunscreen with an **SPF** of 30 or higher. Apply it evenly over all exposed areas. Make sure to reapply sunscreen after swimming or sweating heavily. Avoid the sun during its brightest times, between 10 a.m. and 2 p.m.

You can also treat your skin well from the inside. Drink plenty of water. Eat healthy foods. A balanced diet will give your skin energy to do its job. Make sure to get plenty of rest. Much of your skin's repair work happens while you sleep. Eight hours a night is the right amount for most people.

Most sunscreen creates a physical barrier between the sun and the skin. It protects the skin from sunburn.

Drinking plenty of water will help you stay healthy inside and out. The skin needs water just as much as the rest of the body.

There is only one organ that lets you feel touch. Thanks to your skin, you can feel a soft blanket or the rough bark on a tree. Your skin is the largest part of you. Take care of the skin you are in.

Quiz

1. **What is the internal temperature of a healthy body?**

2. **What is the top layer of your skin called?**

3. **What part of the body has the most nerve endings?**

4. **What is another name for stitches?**

5. **What is the epidermis made of?**

6. **How long does a skin cell live for?**

7. **What substance does your skin make to protect itself from the sun?**

8. **What is a callous?**

9. **What two things does the skin keep away from internal organs?**

10. **What part of the skin house blood vessels, sweat glands, and nerve endings?**

Answers

1. 98.6 degrees Fahrenheit (37 degrees Celsius)
2. The epidermis
3. The fingertips
4. Sutures
5. Dead skin cells
6. About 35 days
7. Melanin
8. An area of skin that is thick and tough
9. Water and germs
10. The dermis

Key Words

antibiotic: a drug used to cure infections and diseases

cells: the smallest unit of a living thing

dermis: an inner layer of living skin cells that contains nerves, glands, and blood vessels

epidermis: the thin outer layer of skin

germs: very small living things that can cause disease

glands: organs that allow substances to leave the body

melanin: a substance in skin that protects it from light

organ: a part of the body that does a particular job

signal: an action or impulse that is used to share information

SPF: sun protection factor

Index

Log on to www.av2books.com

AV² by Weigl brings you media enhanced books that support active learning. Go to www.av2books.com, and enter the special code found on page 2 of this book. You will gain access to enriched and enhanced content that supplements and complements this book. Content includes video, audio, weblinks, quizzes, a slide show, and activities.

AV² Online Navigation

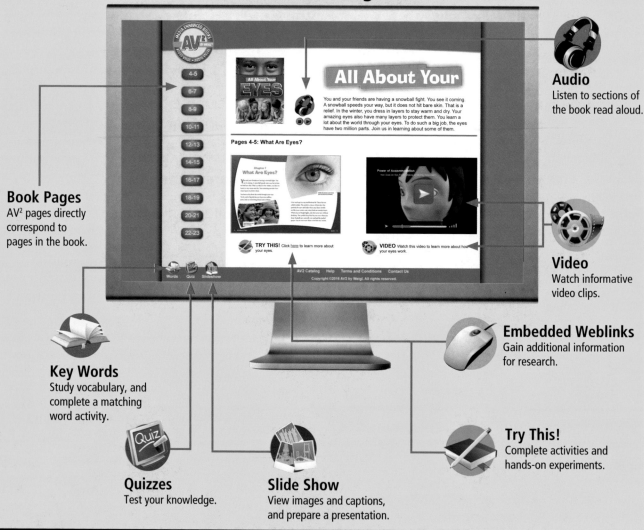

Audio
Listen to sections of the book read aloud.

Video
Watch informative video clips.

Embedded Weblinks
Gain additional information for research.

Try This!
Complete activities and hands-on experiments.

Book Pages
AV² pages directly correspond to pages in the book.

Key Words
Study vocabulary, and complete a matching word activity.

Quizzes
Test your knowledge.

Slide Show
View images and captions, and prepare a presentation.

AV² was built to bridge the gap between print and digital. We encourage you to tell us what you like and what you want to see in the future.

Sign up to be an AV² Ambassador at www.av2books.com/ambassador.

Due to the dynamic nature of the Internet, some of the URLs and activities provided as part of AV² by Weigl may have changed or ceased to exist. AV² by Weigl accepts no responsibility for any such changes. All media enhanced books are regularly monitored to update addresses and sites in a timely manner. Contact AV² by Weigl at 1-866-649-3445 or av2books@weigl.com with any questions, comments, or feedback.